W9-BTH-089

INSIDE STORY

BY MIKE LAMBOURNE
ILLUSTRATIONS BY THOMPSON YARDLEY

INSIDE
STORY

THE MILLBROOK PRESS · BROOKFIELD, CONNECTICUT

Library of Congress Cataloging-in-Publication Data

Lambourne, Mike.
Inside story: the latest news about your body / Mike Lambourne ;
illustrations by Thompson Yardley.
p.   cm.—(A Lighter look book)
Includes bibliographical references and index.
Summary: Explains in lighthearted fashion the workings of the
human body, covering the major organ systems and health tips.
ISBN 1-56294-148-8
1. Human physiology—Juvenile literature. 2. Body, Human—
Juvenile literature. [1. Human physiology. 2. Body, Human.]
I. Hardley, THompson, 1951– ill. II. Title. III. Series.
QP37.L36   1992
612—dc20   91-22960 CIP AC

First published in the United States in 1992 by
The Millbrook Press Inc.
2 Old New Milford Road
Brookfield, Connecticut 06804
© Copyright Cassell plc 1991
First published in Great Britain in 1991 by
Cassell Publishers Limited
6 5 4 3 2 1

INSIDE STORY

WHAT COLOR ARE YOU?

BROWN? PINK?  GREEN?

If you're green, you must be a space alien!
This book is for humans only—so clear off!

Whatever color a person is, all the insides are more or less the same.
Do you know what's inside your body?

Find out . . .

What your bones are for!
Why dreaming is good for you!
What makes you sick!
Why scabs are good for you!

Skin keeps your insides in. But skin is more than just a bag for your insides. It's the largest organ of the body. It works hard to protect your other organs. And it grows!

Fingernails and hair are part of your skin. Hair grows about a quarter of an inch (half a centimeter) a week. Your fingernails grow too, but much more slowly.

CHECK YOUR NAIL GROWTH EXPERIMENT

1. Gather your friends together and get a safety pin each.

SCRITCH!

2. Lightly scratch the first letter of your name on an index fingernail. Don't stab yourself!

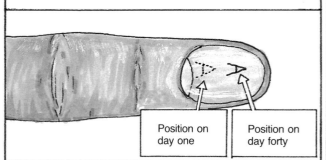

Position on day one

Position on day forty

3. As the nail grows, the letter will seem to move up the nail.

I'm winning!

No! I'm winning!

4. See whose letter disappears off the end first. No cheating—don't bite your nails!

FAIRLY LONG INDIAN THUMBNAIL FACT

A man in India has a thumbnail that's three feet (one meter) long! He hasn't cut his left-hand nails since 1952. They're curved, so he can scratch backs around corners!

A bit to the left!

DEAD SKIN EATERS FACT

Skin wears away and is gradually replaced by new skin. People shed tiny flakes of dead skin everywhere they go. Tiny creatures called dust mites live in houses and eat our dead skin!

Actual size

CHOMP! NIBBLE!

Surface skin is worn away by everyday scratching and scraping. If you've got pale skin, the sun may damage it too. A bad sunburn can make some people's skin peel off in chunks!

AARGH! Too much sun!

Litter lout!

PEEL!

I've got 483 moles and freckles!

If they were all joined up you'd have brown skin like me!

MOLE NOTE-BOOK

Too much sunbathing can also give you skin cancer. Many people have dark skin, which protects them from sunlight. This dark color is a skin chemical called melanin. Fair-skinned people have tiny blobs of melanin scattered all over their bodies. These are called moles!

But don't confuse moles with spots!

DO YOU GET SPOTS??

SILLY SPOT STORY

Your skin is home for millions of tiny bacteria. They like moist areas such as armpits, feet, and between your legs. They feed on sweat, skin oil, and bits of dead skin. Here's a close-up of a small area of skin.

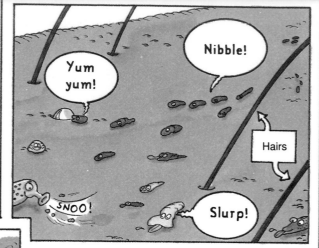

Most of these bacteria are harmless, and some are even helpful to you. They fight off other more dangerous bacteria that try to invade.

Sweat comes out of tiny holes called pores. Pores sometimes become blocked with dirt or old skin oil. This attracts too many invading bacteria for your defending bacteria to fight off.

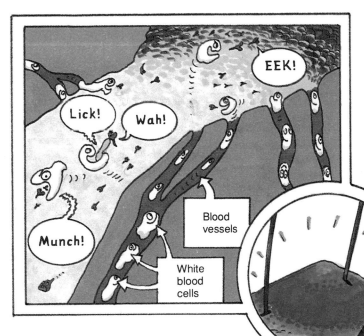

But your body has a second army to defend you. Your blood carries white blood cells to the invasion site. These eat the invading bacteria. The area swells with blood as more blood cells join in. So a red spot forms.

The white blood cells and invading bacteria form a war zone. This is the yellow stuff called pus. Eventually, the invaders are killed off and the skin returns to normal. But don't squeeze spots. This lets bacteria escape and set up home next door!

You have to help your body to fight off invaders. Keep your skin clean with soap and water. Then dab yourself dry with a clean towel. Don't overdo the cleaning— scrubbing too hard damages skin and lets bacteria in!

Of course, the biggest hole in your skin is your mouth!

TYPES OF TEETH

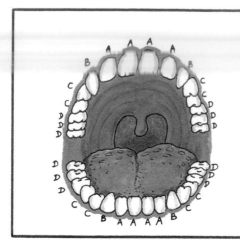

A. Incisors
   cut food
B. Canines
   tear food
C. Premolars
   crush food
D. Molars
   grind food

There are four types of teeth. They each have a particular job to do. As you grow up your teeth change in shape and strength.

MILK TOOTH

Most babies are born without visible teeth. After about six months, small white teeth grow up through the gums. Their roots are quite small.

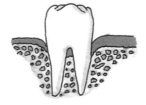

ADULT TOOTH

After about six years, adult teeth start to grow. These have roots in the jawbone. They grow and push out the milk teeth.

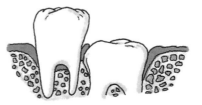

WISDOM TOOTH

After about thirteen years there are usually twenty-eight adult teeth. Between ages thirteen and twenty-one, the last four appear. These late arrivals may squeeze other teeth.

LARGEST TEETH FACT

Teeth aren't just for eating. Some animals use them to fight off other animals. The tusks of elephants are the largest teeth in the world.

SMALLEST TEETH FACT

Nobody knows which animals have the smallest teeth. But some animals have no teeth at all!

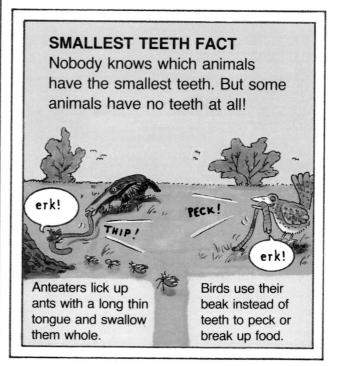

Anteaters lick up ants with a long thin tongue and swallow them whole.

Birds use their beak instead of teeth to peck or break up food.

[12]

DOWN IN THE MOUTH

What's for dinner today?

Yum yum! Caramel toffee!

My favorite!

Bacteria arrive in your mouth from food, water, and air. They eat the tiny bits of food that stick to your teeth. As they eat, they give off acid wastes. These cause holes, called cavities, in your teeth. Then they have to be repaired by a dentist.

SLOOSH!!

Cleaning teeth and gums with a toothbrush and toothpaste scrubs away the food and most of the bacteria.

SCRUB!

Time to go!

Let me out!

eek!

Who's that?

It's Sidney Spitt! He's horrible!

PTOO!

SPITTING IMAGE FACT
The wet stuff in your mouth is called saliva, or spit. It helps you to digest your food. But saliva also carries bacteria. It can pass on colds, flu, and other nasty diseases. So spitting is very unhygienic, as well as being unpleasant to look at.

TRY THIS SLIMY TONGUE TWISTER!
IT MAKES YOU SICK SEEING SIDNEY SPITT SPITTING THICK SPIT!

erk!

TO THE HANDKERCHIEF SHOP

BEING SICK

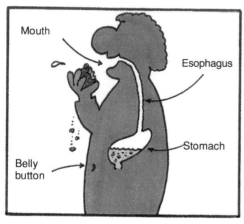

Mouth

Esophagus

Stomach

Belly button

When you eat, your food goes down a tube called the esophagus. This tube leads to your stomach.

As your stomach fills up, your belly sticks out a little bit. Your stomach muscles and skin expand to allow space for the food.

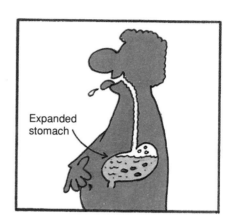

Expanded stomach

Your stomach contains acids that help to digest your food. If you eat too quickly, your stomach expands too quickly. Then you get indigestion.

STALE CAKES

HEY! What's all this junk?

Make sure you eat a variety of fresh foods. Eating a lot of one sort of food, or food that's going bad, is asking for trouble. Your stomach won't like it!

Eating is a pleasant activity. Being sick isn't! That's because it's like eating in reverse. Your stomach muscles squeeze your food back up again. It's a good idea to drink some water after you've been sick. This soothes your stomach and replaces the water you've lost.

Serves you right!

UURRRP!!

WHOOSH!!

TUMMY BUGS

After being partly digested in your stomach, your food is squeezed into your intestines. Two nearby organs called the liver and the pancreas squirt chemicals into your intestines. Food is squeezed by the intestines and digested by the chemicals.

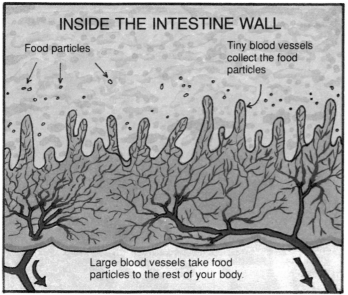

INSIDE THE INTESTINE WALL

Food particles

Tiny blood vessels collect the food particles

Large blood vessels take food particles to the rest of your body.

The small and large intestines form a tube that in adults is about twenty-five feet (seven meters) long!

The walls of your small intestine soak up food. The large intestine soaks up water. Tiny blood vessels take away the digested particles. The nearly solid waste that your body can't use is stored in your rectum until you go to the toilet. Your rectum squeezes the waste out of your anus.

Liver

Stomach

Pancreas

Large Intestine

Rectum

Small intestine

Anus

Sometimes bacteria survive the stomach acids and reach your intestines. Your intestines hate some types of bacteria. They work quickly to get rid of infected food. Then you have to go to the toilet quickly!

Other harmless types of bacteria are always present in your intestines. They produce waste gases that you can sometimes smell.

Dennis! Stop that at once!

It's only bacteria gas, Mom!

PARP!

THE BLOOD SYSTEM

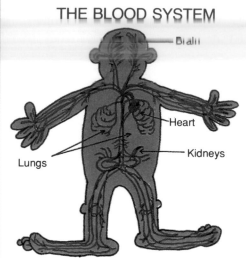

Brain

Heart

Kidneys

Lungs

You can see veins near the surface of your skin. They look blue. Arteries are deeper under your skin and usually can't be seen. In this diagram, the veins are colored blue and arteries are colored red.

There are a huge number of blood vessels in your body. Joined end to end they might stretch twice around the world!

They carry food particles, water, and oxygen to all parts of your body. Arteries carry oxygen from your lungs to your muscles and organs. Veins carry waste products back to your lungs.

WHAT'S IN BLOOD?
Blood has four main parts.

RED BLOOD CELLS

These cells carry oxygen from your lungs and carry wastes back to be breathed out.

WHITE BLOOD CELLS

These attack the bacteria that sometimes invade your body.

PLATELETS

These are sticky little cells that help to block up cuts.

PLASMA
This is a liquid that all the other things float in. It also carries all the useful chemicals from your food to all parts of your body.

"WOW! ALL THAT IN A DROP OF BLOOD!" FACT
Blood cells are incredibly tiny. A small drop of blood contains about . . .

10,000 white cells!
300,000 platelets!
5,000,000 red cells!

WOW!
All that in a drop of blood!

[16]

SCABS!

When you cut yourself, you bleed. But not for long. Your blood cells leap into action to save your body from emptying!

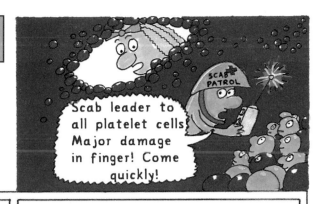

Scab leader to all platelet cells: Major damage in finger! Come quickly!

1. Platelet cells arrive and stick to each other. They form a network across a small cut.

Grunt!

Umph!

Steady!

Left hand down a bit!

Get off my nose!

2. Stringy lumps of chemicals called proteins arrive. They form a network over larger cuts.

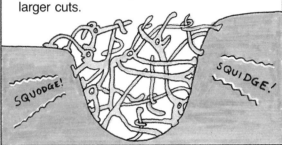

SQUODGE!

SQUIDGE!

3. Red cells arrive and clump together in rolls.

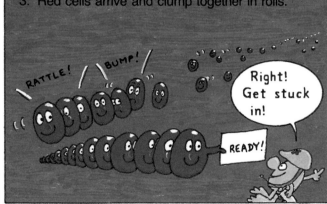

RATTLE!

BUMP!

Right! Get stuck in!

READY!

4. These red cells block up the spaces in the network of platelets.

YIPPEE!

The scab patrol wins again!

Look! A nasty little scab picker!

I'll stop her!

PICKER CATCHER

PICK! PICK!

SCREECH!

The plug of platelets and red cells hardens to form a scab. This helps to keep out bacteria while new skin is growing underneath. Scabs help you to heal up . . . so don't pick them!

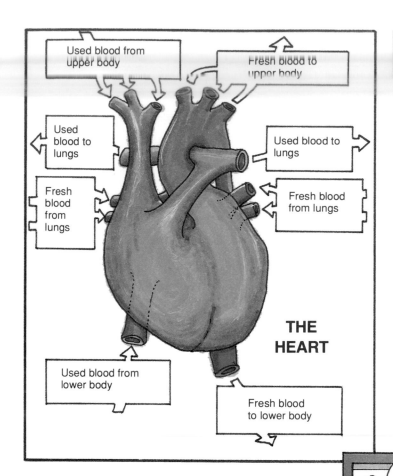

Used blood from upper body

Fresh blood to upper body

Used blood to lungs

Used blood to lungs

Fresh blood from lungs

Fresh blood from lungs

Used blood from lower body

Fresh blood to lower body

THE HEART

This is your heart. It's about the same size and shape as a large pear. Its job is to pump blood around your body. It's actually two pumps in one. The right side (the part toward the right side of your body) pumps used blood from your body to your lungs. The left side pumps fresh blood from your lungs to your body. You can feel the movement of your blood as it's pumped around your body.

CHECK YOUR PULSE EXPERIMENT

The heartbeat you can feel at certain parts of your body is called your pulse. Get a watch and try timing your pulse. Rest your arm on a table and feel for your pulse like this . . .

Your muscles need more blood when you exercise. So your pulse becomes quicker. Try jumping up and down about thirty times. Then check your pulse with a watch again.

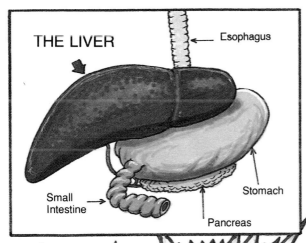

THE LIVER

Esophagus

Small Intestine

Stomach

Pancreas

AMAZING LIVER!

This is your liver. It's a rubbery-looking organ, weighing about three pounds (one-and-a-half kilograms). It doesn't look like much—but liver experts say it does at least five hundred different jobs for your body! It's sometimes called the body's chemical factory, because it . . .

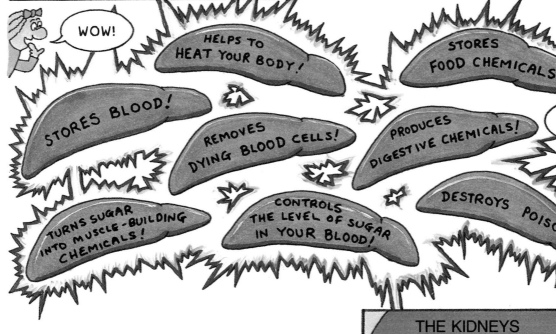

WOW!

HELPS TO HEAT YOUR BODY!

STORES FOOD CHEMICALS!

STORES BLOOD!

REMOVES DYING BLOOD CELLS!

PRODUCES DIGESTIVE CHEMICALS!

WOW!

TURNS SUGAR INTO MUSCLE-BUILDING CHEMICALS!

CONTROLS THE LEVEL OF SUGAR IN YOUR BLOOD!

DESTROYS POISONS!

AMAZING KIDNEYS!

You also have two kidneys. They have the job of filtering the blood that flows through them. They pick out chemical wastes and mix them with water. This mixture, called urine, collects in your bladder. When your bladder is full, it tells your brain. Then you know it's time to go to the toilet!

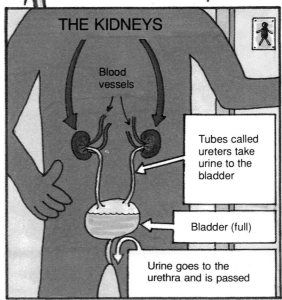

THE KIDNEYS

Blood vessels

Tubes called ureters take urine to the bladder

Bladder (full)

Urine goes to the urethra and is passed

MUSCLES

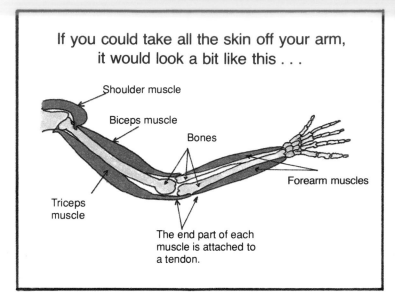

If you could take all the skin off your arm,
it would look a bit like this . . .

Shoulder muscle

Biceps muscle

Bones

Triceps muscle

Forearm muscles

The end part of each muscle is attached to a tendon.

ROMAN MOUSE MUSCLE FACT

SQUEAK!

The word "muscle" comes from the Roman word for mouse. Flex your arm muscles. You'll see your upper arm muscle moving under your skin like a mouse in a bag!

There are muscles all over your body. The big ones are all connected to your bones. Smaller muscles, such as face muscles, are often connected to each other.

Here's a simplified diagram of how your upper arm muscles work . . .

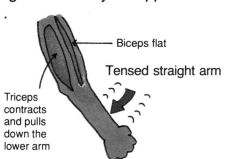

Biceps flat

Tensed straight arm

Triceps contracts and pulls down the lower arm

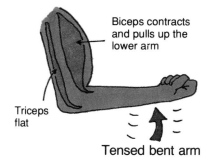

Biceps contracts and pulls up the lower arm

Triceps flat

Tensed bent arm

TOUGH TENDON TEST

The thin end parts of a muscle are called tendons. They are very tough. They grip your bones and pull when your muscle contracts. You can see a thumb tendon working when you hold your hand like this . . .

Place the palm of your hand flat on a table. Lift your thumb off the table and watch your thumb tendon moving.

1. Get a bathroom scale and put it on a table.

2. Sit on a chair and rest your hand on the scale like this.

3. Press down on the scale and feel your triceps pulling.

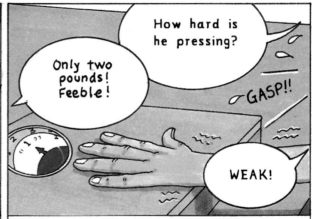

4. Read the scale. How much pressure does your arm produce?

You'll find your arm gets tired after only a few seconds. If you tried this experiment every day for a month, your arm would get bigger and stronger. Don't overdo it, or your muscles may grow too much!

But . . . why do muscles get tired?

HOT MUSCLES

Muscles are made of millions of tiny cells. Each long thin cell is attached to other cells. As each cell contracts or relaxes, your muscle contracts and relaxes too. Blood vessels bring oxygen and sugar to feed each cell. Other blood vessels take away waste products.

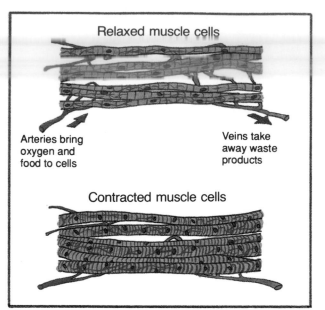

Relaxed muscle cells

Arteries bring oxygen and food to cells

Veins take away waste products

Contracted muscle cells

GOING JOGGING? . . .

1. If you trot, your lungs take in enough oxygen. And your liver sends plenty of sugar to your muscles.

WOW! Stop!

BOING!

2. If you run faster, your muscle cells need more energy. You breathe more quickly, and your heart beats faster to send more blood.

Six miles later . . .

GASP! WHEEZE!

RIP!

WOBBLE!

3. If you run for too long, waste products build up. This stops the cells from working properly. They become weak or jammed in one position. Then you get a "stitch" or cramp.

PUFF! PANT!

GASP!!

4. Your heart can't beat fast enough to clear the blockages. Your muscles hurt. You feel wobbly. You stop and pant for breath!

COLD MUSCLES

The more exercise your muscles get, the healthier they become. That's why top athletes train every day. But they always stretch and do gentle exercises before they start. This warms up their muscles so that their blood flows more easily.

Some athletes stretching!

TRY THIS . . .

1. Get a piece of cold modeling clay. Pull it apart quickly. It breaks!

2. Put the pieces back together. Roll the lump in your hands until it's warm. Pull it apart—now it stretches!

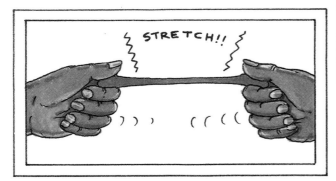

Cold muscles can be damaged by stretching them too quickly. Always warm up before playing sports, especially on cold days.

Sometimes your muscles ache after hard exercise. When you've finished, keep your muscles warm. This helps your blood to flow, taking away the wastes that build up in tired muscles.

Bones have three main jobs to do.

BONES MAKE BLOOD CELLS
The long bone in your thigh is called a femur. The soft marrow in the center produces blood cells. Other bones make blood cells too.

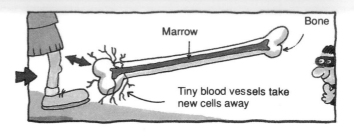

Marrow

Bone

Tiny blood vessels take new cells away

HAH!

Hmmph!

BONES

BONES GIVE YOU A SHAPE
Imagine if somebody stole your bones! Your muscles would have nothing to pull on. You'd flop down in a heap!

PONK!

BLLP!

WOP!

With a skull

Without a skull!

BONES PROTECT YOU
Bones protect your organs from injury. For example, your tough skull bones protect your brain.

COUNT YOUR BONES QUIZ!

Bones are usually attached to each other at flexible parts called joints. For example, three bones meet at your elbow joint.
See if you can count all your bones!

In a leg?

In an arm?

Inside an ear??

Answer: Legs have thirty, arms have thirty, and each ear has three. You can't see your ear bones because they're inside your skull. In fact, it's impossible to count all your bones without using an X-ray machine. There are two hundred and six altogether.

BROKEN BONES

Bones are made of a mixture of two materials. One material is hard and makes bones strong. The other material is rubbery to make bones flexible.

YOUNG BONES
Young bones have more of the rubbery material.
They bend a long way before they break.

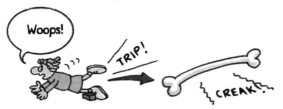

OLD BONES
Older people's bones have more of the hard material.
They break more easily.

Fortunately, broken bones usually heal up quite well. But young bones heal up quicker than old bones. A doctor wraps a damaged bone in a solid plaster cast to keep it still. This helps it to mend straight. The cast is taken off later.

You can see how a plaster cast helps when you try this

BROKEN BRANCH EXPERIMENT!

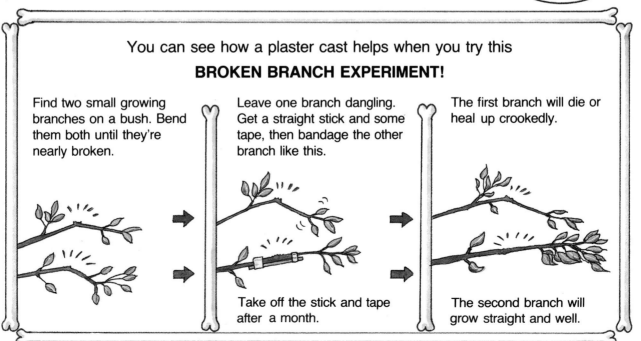

Find two small growing branches on a bush. Bend them both until they're nearly broken.

Leave one branch dangling. Get a straight stick and some tape, then bandage the other branch like this.

The first branch will die or heal up crookedly.

Take off the stick and tape after a month.

The second branch will grow straight and well.

That's why we can heal up!

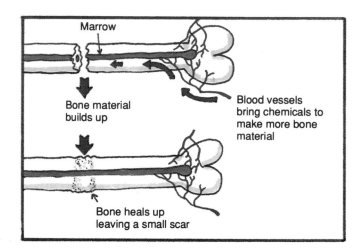

Marrow

Bone material builds up

Bone heals up leaving a small scar

Blood vessels bring chemicals to make more bone material

Bone marrow produces blood cells that are taken away by blood vessels. These blood vessels also bring chemicals from the rest of your body to make more bone. This bone material fills up the gap between parts of the broken bone.

Bread

Fish

Cheese

Milk

The two main chemicals in bones are calcium and phosphorus. These are found in your food. All of these foods are good for your bones.

COSMONAUT BONE FACT

The more you exercise your bones, the stronger they get. Your bones support your body, so you get some exercise just by standing up! But . . . in outer space, there's no gravity, so bones don't get much exercise. Soviet cosmonauts often spend a long time in space. Their bones get weaker and weaker!

Ivan! Come back in quick! Your leg's just fallen off!

SPORTSBONES!

You need to treat your bones like pets. Feed and exercise them. Walking is good for bones!

But watch out! Too much exercise is bad for growing bones. Be extra careful if you take up weight lifting!

Jogging is very popular these days. But if you run on hard pavements you may hurt yourself. If you want to jog, do it in a park where the ground is soft and springy.

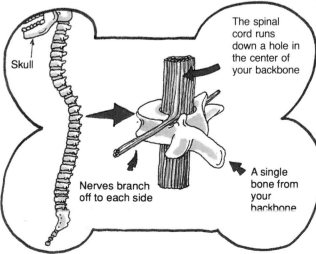

Your backbone isn't a single bone at all. It's a chain of twenty-six small bones linked together. It's strong enough to support your body. And it's flexible enough to bend in all sorts of different directions. And it has another job to do—it protects your spinal cord!

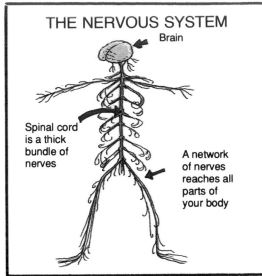

THE NERVOUS SYSTEM

Brain

Spinal cord is a thick bundle of nerves

A network of nerves reaches all parts of your body

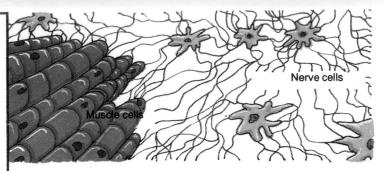

Nerve cells

Muscle cells

Your body is made up of millions of tiny cells. Nerve cells are special because they can pass on messages from the brain to all the other cells. Nerve cells help the brain to control the other cells too. It works a bit like this . . .

Nice pussy!

STROKE!

GNASH!

YOW!

Each nerve cell is part of a network that passes on orders from your brain.

The chain of nerves also sends messages back to your brain.

Your brain works all the time to solve difficult problems!

ALL IN YOUR HEAD!

There are nerves in your skin so you can feel things that touch or hurt you. And your eyes, ears, nose, and tongue have nerves that can send messages. For example your nose can "feel" smells and your tongue can "feel" tastes!

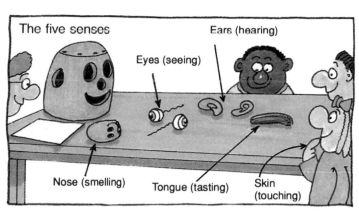

The five senses

Eyes (seeing)

Ears (hearing)

Nose (smelling)

Tongue (tasting)

Skin (touching)

Derek! Where are you!

What? I can't hear!

Most of these special nerve groups are in your head. That's so you can sense things better. Think what it would be like having eyes and ears on your feet!

Different parts of your brain have different jobs to do. And the senses are mostly in your head so as to be close to your brain. This means that messages can be passed on as quickly as possible.

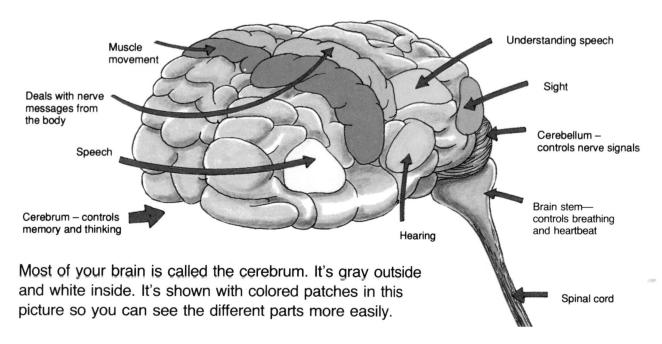

Muscle movement

Deals with nerve messages from the body

Speech

Cerebrum – controls memory and thinking

Understanding speech

Sight

Cerebellum – controls nerve signals

Brain stem— controls breathing and heartbeat

Hearing

Spinal cord

Most of your brain is called the cerebrum. It's gray outside and white inside. It's shown with colored patches in this picture so you can see the different parts more easily.

WHAT A BRAIN!

Your brain is a bit like a very powerful computer. It processes information and comes up with answers. The main difference is that your brain is conscious —it can decide what it wants to do. Some scientists are trying to invent computers that behave like the human brain!

Your brain has a huge memory, but it's often not as accurate as a computer. Your brain stores memories away in a sort of mental library. Memories you need every day are easy to find, like popular books. Memories you don't use much are cobwebby and hard to find.

A BRAINTEASER QUIZ—HOW GOOD IS YOUR MEMORY?

Look at these nine body parts for a minute, then cover them up.
See if you can remember their positions.

1. What's above the foot?
2. What's in the bottom left corner?
3. Is the ear on the middle line?
4. What's in the middle of the top line?
5. What's below the nose?

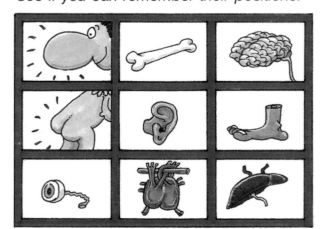

How did you do?

5 = Brain!
4 = Good!
3 = Quite good!
2 = Try again!
1 = Brain transplant needed!!

NERVE POISONS

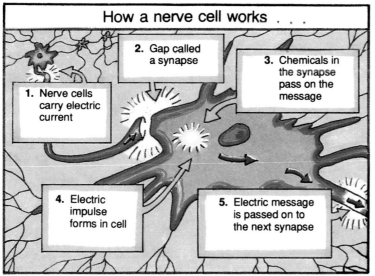

How a nerve cell works . . .

1. Nerve cells carry electric current

2. Gap called a synapse

3. Chemicals in the synapse pass on the message

4. Electric impulse forms in cell

5. Electric message is passed on to the next synapse

The messages passing through nerve cells are tiny electric currents. But nerve cells aren't joined to each other. There's a gap between each cell. This gap is called a synapse. Chemicals released by the first cell pass on messages across the synapse to the next cell in the chain.

Some poisons work by interfering with the chemicals in the synapses. For example, some bacteria produce poisons that stop messages from crossing synapses. A victim of these bacteria may be unable to move! But some substances make nerve messages move faster. Caffeine will "wake you up" by speeding up the synapse chemicals.

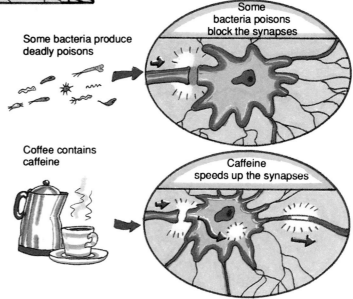

Some bacteria produce deadly poisons

Some bacteria poisons block the synapses

Coffee contains caffeine

Caffeine speeds up the synapses

Doctors say that alcohol and the nicotine in tobacco are poisonous drugs. These substances interfere with nerve cells. Nervous or tense people like to use these drugs to calm themselves down. But alcohol can also make people clumsy! And tobacco affects smokers too. They can't breathe properly!

[31]

TAKE A BREATHER!

Breathing in draws air into your lungs. Air contains oxygen. You need oxygen to make your muscles work.

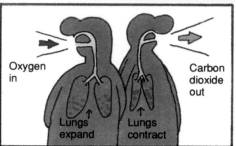

Oxygen in

Carbon dioxide out

Lungs expand

Lungs contract

The air you breathe out contains unwanted carbon dioxide from your muscles. Tobacco smoke contains carbon dioxide too!

Your lungs aren't like inflatable bags. They're more like two damp, pink sponges!

Windpipe

Lungs

Blood vessels

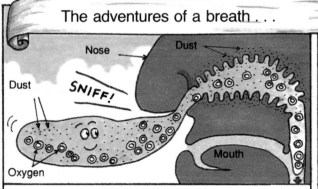

The adventures of a breath . . .

Nose

Dust

Dust

SNIFF!

Mouth

Oxygen

1. Air goes into your nose and down your windpipe. Tiny blood vessels warm it up. Sticky stuff called mucus cleans it of dust.

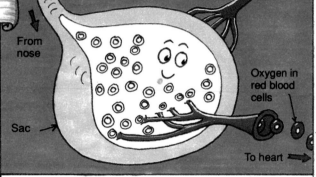

From nose

Sac

Oxygen in red blood cells

To heart

2. Your lungs contain 750 million tiny sacs connected to blood vessels. Red blood cells soak up the oxygen and take it to your heart.

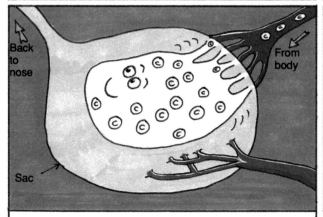

Back to nose

From body

Sac

3. Your heart pumps the red cells around your body. Your blood collects carbon dioxide from your muscles and returns it to your lungs.

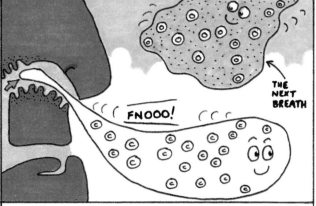

THE NEXT BREATH

FNOOO!

4. You breathe out the waste gas . . . and breathe in again!

UP YOUR NOSE!

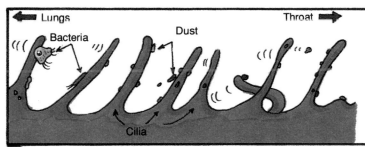

Your windpipe contains millions of tiny hairlike things called cilia. Their job is to pick out dust and bacteria from the air you breathe. These bits of stuff are passed on up to your throat.

I think I'll get her a hanky for Christmas!

COUGHING

Dust and bacteria collect in your windpipe and nose. If enough dirty mucus builds up quickly, it has to be removed quickly before you choke. That's why you cough. If you need to cough, face away from other people so as not to spread bacteria.

SNEEZING

Sneezing spreads bacteria too. A powerful sneeze can shoot particles from your nose at 100 mph (160 kph)! Another interesting thing is that you can't keep your eyes open when you sneeze. Try it and see. Look where you're going if you feel a sneeze coming on!

There's a good bit up there somewhere!

Yuk! He's horrible!

Snot is mucus that has nearly dried up. Almost everybody picks their nose, but most people think it looks bad. So they do it in secret! But eating it really is bad. Snot is full of dirt and germs that your nose has stopped from getting into your body!

THE BACK-TO-FRONT BODY PARTS QUIZ

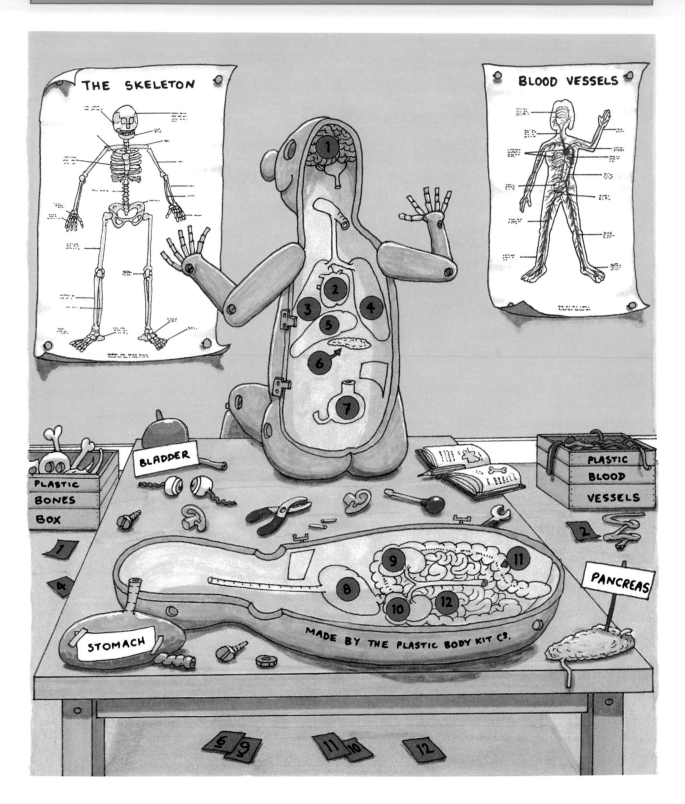

Tense muscles can give you a backache or a headache.
Breathing and relaxing properly makes you feel better.

TRY THIS . . .

1. Sit cross-legged against a wall. Close your eyes. Let your arms hang loose. Let your chin droop to your chest.

2. Breathe in deeply through your nose. Hold it for a few seconds. Breathe out slowly.

3. Repeat this for a few minutes. Relax the muscles in your face, neck, and shoulders.

4. Of course if you relax completely, you may nod off!

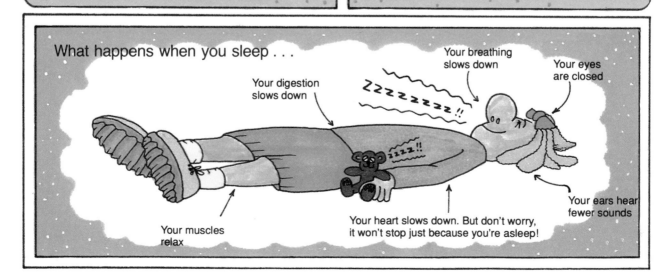

What happens when you sleep . . .

Your breathing slows down

Your eyes are closed

Your digestion slows down

Your heart slows down. But don't worry, it won't stop just because you're asleep!

Your ears hear fewer sounds

Your muscles relax

SWEET DREAMS

Most of your body slows down when you sleep. But one part doesn't. Your brain never stops working! When you sleep, only part of it switches off. Another part keeps your body alive. The rest of your brain relaxes by inventing dreams. Dreams can sometimes be very strange!

Dreaming is important. While you dream, your brain rummages through the day's events and puts everything in order. People who don't get enough sleep have a poor memory and get angry easily. Most young people need seven to ten hours of sleep each night. Your brain gets very grumpy if you don't give it enough sleep!

Your body carries you along from when you were born to perhaps a hundred years into the future!

The more you know about what goes on inside, the better you can

LOOK AFTER YOUR BODY!

You won't get another one!

FIND OUT MORE

Now that you've read the latest news about your body, you may want to learn more about the way it works. Here are some books to look for in the library:

Blood, by Herbert S. Zim (Morrow, 1968)

Blood and Guts: A Working Guide to Your Own Insides, by Linda Allison (Little Brown, 1976)

The Brain and Nervous System, by Steve Parker (Watts, 1990)

The Human Body, by Ruth D. Bruun and Bertel Bruun (Random House, 1982)

The Macmillan Book of the Human Body, by Mary Elting (Macmillan, 1986)

The Magic School Bus: Inside the Human Body, by Joanna Cole (Scholastic, 1989)

Outside and Inside You, by Sandra Markle (Bradbury, 1991)

Your Skin, by Herbert S. Zim (Morrow, 1979)

INDEX